How I Enjoy Trading Stocks Online

The Principles of
Cognitive Perception and Intuition

MANUEL T. PROSPERO, MD

AuthorHouse™
1663 Liberty Drive
Bloomington, IN 47403
www.authorhouse.com
Phone: 1-800-839-8640

© 2012 by Manuel T. Prospero, MD. All rights reserved.

No part of this book may be reproduced, stored in a retrieval system, or transmitted by any means without the written permission of the author.

Published by AuthorHouse   04/23/2012

ISBN: 978-1-4685-6384-9 (sc)
ISBN: 978-1-4685-6383-2 (e)

Any people depicted in stock imagery provided by Thinkstock are models, and such images are being used for illustrative purposes only.
Certain stock imagery © Thinkstock.

This book is printed on acid-free paper.

Because of the dynamic nature of the Internet, any web addresses or links contained in this book may have changed since publication and may no longer be valid. The views expressed in this work are solely those of the author and do not necessarily reflect the views of the publisher, and the publisher hereby disclaims any responsibility for them.

Disclaimer

The author is not responsible for any losses resulting from investment decisions based on the use of the book. In no event shall this book be liable for any special, incidental or consequential damages, including without limitations, damages, for loss of profit, monetary loss and others arising out of this book.

All contents provided should be used solely as educational guide and not as an investment advice on what stocks to buy.

No part of this book, may be reproduced or transmitted by any means, photocopying, recording or otherwise, without written permission from the Author.

The book is based on my experience, and using informations available to me as references. However, it is not intended to be guarantees of any future endeavors and effort to succeed in the market.

Free Market Capitalism and the Path To Prosperity

The Market Averages

The Dow Jones Industrial Averages—An average number of 30 major blue chip companies trading on the New York Stock Exchange. The Standard & Poor's 500—A group of 500 widely traded stocks. It represents the market more than the Dow that consists only of 30 big well established stocks. The Nasdaq Composite Index includes over 5,000 companies and is the most widely followed.

They are the direct image of our economy. These are the DOW, Nasdaq, and S&P 500 indexes. Charles Dow was the founder of Dow Jones and Company and created an index of 30 big companies. This was the <u>Dow Jones Industrial average in **1895.**</u> It served as an **indicator** of <u>business activity </u>as we <u>started using and forecasting stock price movements.</u>

In **1897**, he created an average index for <u>railroad stocks</u> that will later become the Dow Jones Transportation Index, and later came the Dow Jones Utility Index.

Manuel T. Prospero, MD

The U.S. Economic System

The United States is a country whose economic system is based on <u>free enterprise</u>, the corporate America. This is a system in which the businesses are owned <u>privately.</u> The owners and workers are <u>free</u> to use their resources, energies, efforts, newer innovations as they desire. They are not owned by the government but by private individuals or corporations. When I buy a stock of a company, I am actually buying a part of the company. Democratic countries believe that capitalism and free enterprise are the best path to prosperity.

Successful American innovators like Jeff Bezos of Amazon the first online bookstore, and the late Steve Job of Apple, Bill Gates of Microsoft, all started in the 60s. Google was first incorporated in 1998 founded by Larry Page and Sergey Brinn, and before them we already have successful companies like Boeing, Caterpillar, IBM, and many mid and small cap companies. Today we have the young Mike Zuckerberg of Facebook, a public social networking company.

A Brief Walk in the Stock Market

As an investor, we always try to look for the best growth stocks and hold on to them for as long as we can for profit. But this is no longer true because of the current uncertainty and volatility in the market, brought about by slow economic growth in the U.S. (2009-2011) and European countries debt crisis. At the present time, the market is not a place for investors with a long term horizon.

Some of us are short term investors involved in day and swing trading. However, many of us are still long term value investors. Ex. Small investors can buy a company at its initial public offering and grow forward with the company. A share of Apple, on Dec.1982 was $ 22.00 per share. The stock has split 3 times. As of March 13, 2012, the price is $ 557.08/share.

Venture capitalists provides big start up capital (financing) to innovators with high growth potentials. Most of these capitalists are in Silicon Valley, California.

Usually the founders together with other partners, constitute the management team, committed to their initial idea.

Home Online Trading

Let us clear up some thoughts in the true meaning and nature of home online trading.

Trading is perceiving, buying stocks and hoping that prices will yield us profit if positioned correctly. When we roll the dice or flip the card with our thumb and fingers, on a Casino table, we are speculating and gambling. Gambling is a game of chance. Speculating is a hunch and a creativity in our mind trying to tell us something. On the other hand, trading is looking at various parameters available to us in the Internet. We have the advantage of analyzing and studying them and if done right is very satisfying.

Trading in the comfort of your own home. You are your own boss. Online brokerage services are available even globally Thanks to the brokerage internet's—based proprietary trading platforms. Even retirees are capable of doing this in their computers.

The daily current news about our economy is now available to us at the touch of our fingers. We can educate ourselves and learn a lot from the Internet. A self study, just like how many years in college did to us. Education comes in various ways. You **can make a living with formal education, but sometimes passion, on what we want to accomplish can be more rewarding.**

In today's modern technology, we can watch our investment anywhere, even at work. I see people at some fast food eatery in front of their wireless laptop and iPad during lunch breaks. You can monitor your investment portfolio all the time.

Wifi connection is available in almost any location. Wifi system is the ability to wirelessly connect to the Internet through the courtesy of business entities like hospitals, restaurants, hotels and others.

One time, I was confronted by a friend who made a significant mistake in trading and lost money. He said," I am very disappointed and I need your advice"

"Shall I stop trading?" I answered, of course NOT. "You just spent $ 500 educating yourself, consider that as an investment, instead of spending it in a slot or roulet machine in Casinos.

If you follow the different hypothesis and principles mentioned in this book, you will be surprised as to what you can explore and perhaps accomplish.

Wall Street
The New York Stock Exchange

The market is a huge playing field, **the players take the risk and protect their assets all the time.** These are **trading derivatives, commonly known as proprietary trading such as:**

Options, swaps, futures, and other trading strategies mainly by big investment banks. These are compensating moves in order to restrict losses. There are also numerous profit takers and short sellers.

We also have arbitrage trading, a simultaneous buying and selling of stocks or bonds in different markets. They profit on the difference between the prices normally occurring in such markets.

We win and sometimes we lose money the same way as the other investors.

The investing titans like Warren Buffet, George Soros, Jim Rogers, Bill Gross of Pimco, John Paulson, Larry Fink of Block Rock Hedge Fund, and other big players from time to time reduces their stakes in their portfolio. They are willing to yield and accept losses but over the stretch of time find themselves still ahead. Most of them are long term investors.

Things have turned out best for them because for every wrong move they made in the market, they discard it as a step towards moving forward.

Why Do Some Of Us Trade?

As of January 2012, money in the bank's annual earning is almost next to nothing., notwithstanding that our economy has already recovered <u>slowly</u> from the recession and market—crash of **2009.** The unrealistic <u>losses</u> in the pension plans, 401 K retirement accounts (SEP, IRA, Roth) of hardworking Americans, house foreclosures, unemployment, is still a big problem in our economy. Most of us who were self-managing their retirement accounts prior to that market collapse survived and avoided severe losses. There were many scams exposed by the SEC during this time. Ex. Robert Allen Stanford and Bernard Madoff's 50 billions ponzi schemes exposed during that stock market meltdown. The investors may never get their money back.

If you are a good online trader, any amount of capital invested in stocks, can earn you **1% to 4%** in just a few minutes if done correctly. It can be a part time income to some of us and a means of livelihood to others trading on the floor of the stock exchange. Ex. On January of 2012, before the release of Apple's earning after hours, I bought 10 share of the stock. It was already expensive and I took the risk. I had that feeling that its earning will be good. I bought it at $420.63/ share and I sold it form $ 433.18 per share in just a few minutes when it started trading again after being halted.

I bought Apple stock again, when it came out with their new I-Pad 3. I bought shares of Apple at $ 528.00/ share. There are many good stocks we can trade and make money from time to time. We just have to be patient and disciplined.

An $8,000 CD in the bank currently yielding 1.08% per year or .0108, will only earn $86.40/year. Even if compounded every month or yearly, still the return is very low. In 2012, the Fed chairman announced that it will keep down the Federal Funds Rate to zero up to 2014, a pretty stunning news not good for CDs and Money Market accounts. The Fed Rate is tied directly to the movement of short-term interest rates. Ex. The 90-day treasury bill rate.

The Fed Funds rate represents the fundamental cost of credit, the interest rate. This is the interest rate that commercial banks charge each other in overnight borrowing.

They say that most of us are not professional traders and cannot compete with the professionals. This was yesterday, today it is different. Many things have changed in the information and communication technology.

I remember in 1987 crash, my daughter called me on my pager about the market. I had to go to Dean Witter, an investment brokerage firm, to redeem my holdings. Today at the touch of our fingers, we can liquidate our assets in just a few minutes.

The AMERICAN DREAM

After World War II, America became the number one world power economically and militarily. Europe and Asia were both devastated. Everybody would like to come and explore **their future in the United States.** One of the American dreams is to own a house. Owning a house is a great way to save for one's future retirement because real estate increases in value every year and no one lose money. With other business ventures, everybody did well too. In healthcare, more doctors are needed especially in rural areas.

It is because of this American dream, that we migrated to the United States in 1978, with 3 of our small children hoping to make it. It was tough, hard, and challenging to comply with the U.S. requirements and regulations related to our profession. We first settled down in the small town of Foreman, North Dakota with 500 population. Then we moved next to the town of Hankinson with 800 population and finally ended up at Lisbon, with a 3,000 population. We finally found jobs and settled in Chicago.

The Real Estate Market

In the 90s, various real estate business surfaced like NO MONEY Down, Rich/Poor Dad seminars and many more.

Subprime mortgages meaning below normal prime were introduced by the banks to homebuyers. Adjustable rate mortgage was very popular, low monthly payments, approvals with no income verification and other ways to qualify home buyers.

Fannie May and Freddie Mac

Fannie May, the Federal National Mortgage Association was founded in 1938 after the great depression of **1929.** Freddie Mac is a semi-private entity.

Both work with mortgage lenders and help people get a lower housing cost.

They are also <u>secondary</u> buyers of home mortgages. They bundled these home loans and sold as FNM and FRE in the stock market. They were considered very safe and rated tripple AAA, the best the U.S. can offer, guarranteed and backed by the U.S. government.

Investment Banks like Citi group, Lehmann Brothers, Bank of America and other big banks through their respective branches worldwide participated too. The balance sheet of these big investment banks were filled with too many real estate assets before the market collapsed.

"The BOOM"

The bright light in the 80s and early part of **1990** was a general sense of joy and accomplishment brought about by the wonders of the Internet and information technology. Even a bar tender or taxi cab driver with no experience whatsoever in the stock market can make money.

"The BUST"

In Silicon Valley California, emerged most of the dot.com companies. There was a boom in the dot.com business. Nasdaq peaking 5,132.52 points at one time.

Then came the bust in **March 10, 2000.** There were many speculative failures. and it led to the dot com bubbles covering the period from **1995-2000**.

The Economic Cycle

Do the right things on every business cycle and everything will be all right.

The cycle is a recurring period of time where certain event repeat themselves in the same order, intervals, but never exactly the same. However, the stock meltdown of **2009**, involving the housing and credit market, was a different event. It started surfacing in **2007** and resulted into another economic consequence almost similar to the **1929** U.S. economic depression.

It affected lending institution's ability to infuse additional capital to borrowers for economic growth and expansion. Then came the market greatest dip, on **March 9, 2009** the **Dow** went down to **6,544 points** a painful memory to many of us.

The U.S. Financial Crisis and Housing Bubble (2008-2009)

The housing bubble originated from many sophisticated financial-investment product that U.S. financial institutions theoretically and actually introduced globally. As a result, more engagement of U.S. capital circulated to other countries. U.S. mortgage-back securities were sold around the world as far as **Iceland.** One municipality in **Norway** called **Nordic**, bought a lot of these securities thinking that being tripled AAA, is good for their municipality's investment.

Most of the U.S. big banks wrote down their losses. They pay less taxes or NO taxes at all to the government because of such unexpected disaster. These amounted to billions of dollars. This is probably the protesters slogan in **occupy Wall Street in October of 2011, that spread out globally.**

As the U.S. housing buble burst, many of our big banking institutions were at the brink of collapse. To remember this anytime and be prepared for another such cycle is one of the most effectual means of how we can protect our hard earned money.

Freddie Mac and Fannie Mae were extensively involved. Lehmann Brothers filed for bankruptcy, Bear Sterns failed, and on Sept. 19, 2008, the Fed Govt. under the Republican administration, gave the first biggest bail out money to lending institutions and investment banks worth **$ 799** billion dollars. There were rampant bargain hunting, in Wall Street.

Bank of America acquiring Merril Lynch and Countrywide Financial's assets which will later be a problem. In Dec.2011, Bank of America have to pay the Dept. of Justice $ 330 millions, because of Countrywide's lending practices.

Likewise, Warren Buffet increased his stake at Goldman Sach. He is a cyclical value investor and will wait again for the economy to recover as he always did.

During this time, big banks lost their liquid capital assets to lend money. It even became worse when these banks stopped borrowing from each other (short loans). Trust became an issue. Bank money became unavailable. As of March 09, 2012 we are still under the shadow of that crisis although our economy has shown slow recovery. Unemployment rate dropped down to **8.3%**.

Other Factors Affecting Our Investments

U.S. Possible Credit Default

In **August of 2011,** to avoid U.S. credit default, Congress raised the Debt Ceiling. It raised the limit of the money we can borrow and just pay interest on loans. Prior to this date, Standard & Poor (Moody's) downgraded the credit rating of the United States. China owned most of our bonds. Ex. A bond is a debt security, in which the issuer (U.S.) owes the holder (China) a debt and depending on the terms of the bond lended. We are obligated to pay only interest and the principal at a later date. We have **15 trillion dollars of debt w**ith China and other countries.

Moody's is an international accounting specialist group that does financial, credit analysis and credit trustworthiness of countries. Some European countries were at the brink of defaulting like Greece, Spain, Portugal and even Italy. They cannot meet their obligation on their loans with other countries. Greece leaders proposed a bail out referendum on their debt crisis problem. However, severe austerity measures were necessary for the European Union and International

Monetary fund to give Greece a massive bailout to prevent the country from defaulting. This will include massive layoff of public workers. This rattled the markets globally. The U.S. market was down big.

As of this writing, the European Debt Crisis remain unaverted, affecting financial stability of other European nations. If Europe starts printing more money, it will weaken the dollar and in the long term, will affect our economy. When a country defaults on its debts, it can no longer attract foreign investors. Their working capital soon dries up.

In November 12, 2011 Italy's Prime Minister Berlusconi resigned as part of Italy's economic reform.

The Pinhead Politicians

The primary and root cause of unemployment (**2008-2011**) are the housing and real estate problems. The government must find a way to solve this. The values of homes keep going down while property taxes continue to go up. Our government could have done something about this problems after bailing out the big banks in **2008,** with tax payer's money. Instead, they concentrated on the Obama Health Care, Dodd & Frank bank reform and other infrastructure projects. Home prices still have to stabilize.

Those who bought their house 25 years ago, believing that it will be their life savings were devastated. For God's sake, it is the housing market!!! Property tax must be lowered and adjusted accordingly. Homeowners are paying their mortgages on their house with NO equity.

To both Democrats and Republicans . . . . The ability to compromise, is a token of greatness, nothing great will ever be achieved without great men surrounding the President and helping him. And they are great only if they <u>are determined to be so.</u> They are always bitterly divided in many cases. They should solve deep partisan differences on many issues for the sake of the American people. A bipartisan Congress and Senate, and a good Fiscal policy may solve our problems in this fragile economy.

Volatility and Uncertainty in the Market

The President maybe a brilliant and intelligent person, but he is surrounded by political appointees. Some of them may not be fully qualified to give the right advice to the President on many issues confronting our government.

The fall out of making bad bets by the government infrastructure projects are now being exposed prior to 2012 election. These are government loans, that finances new companies even if they are not qualified and viable to continue.

We have several trillion dollars in debt with other countries, increasing and ticking every seconds. The bottom line, we need money to run our government.

On January 13, 2012, S & P downgraded some European countries eight months after we were. Euro as a currency is in big trouble and maybe at the edge of an unfortunate situation. Any market sell off in Europe will indirectly affect our market.

On March 9, 2012, at 2:00 PM Friday (Central Time) <u>Greece</u> had officially defaulted on its debt to private lenders.

As a result, it **changes the way we invest in the market.**

Occupy Wallstreet Protesters

With unemployment of **9.2%**, in **2010-2011, and 8.3% in** early **2012,** we still have a huge budget deficit, the protesters are fed up and scared of how their lives can be lived forward. The Fed keeps on printing money. Our debt to GDP ratio is high and still going up. We are generating more debts than growth. Gross domestic product is the nation's total output of goods and services produced by labor and property located within the borders of the United States.

Two third (2/3) of our overall growth is supported by household investing.

<u>Retail sales</u> accounts for about 1/2 of all household spending, representing 1/3 of the nation's economy and comprise about 1/5 of our gross domestic products.

When the minds of many can no longer believe and trust our two party systems, something must be wrong. I still believe that human beings are still good at heart. They have a darn good reason to object and disapprove of how the White House is handling our government.

The poor and middle class livelihood were affected. When billions of dollars are out there to be spent, corruption and fraud is inevitable like in many third world countries.

Senator McCain, was outraged, and said, "Executives at FNM and Freddie Mac snags millions of bonuses ".

The protester said, that brokerages and investment bankers have manipulated our economy. A Greek doctor once told me "Greece is a socialistic government and almost everything in that country is free."

History tells us that the U.S. being a democratic and capitalistic country, was able to recover from the great depression of 1929 and other succeeding recessions thereafter. Luckily we always went back from where we were in the past.

How To Earn Money In Main Street by Trading Online

Types of Investments:

1.) Short Term Investments are online Day trading and Swing **trading.**

2.) Bond Investments are fixed income investment.

3.) Intermediate and Long term i**nvestments**—Involves mostly Mutual Funds and Index Funds. This long term investment may not be good for many retirement accounts. In March 2009, after the market was down flat to the floor, most of the pension funds suffered. Today (Feb. 2012) most of them are no longer fully funded.

There are two primary ways to stock selection: Fundamental assessment and technical analysis. The former involved the analysis of the company itself like earnings and dividends, current balance sheet and other measures of value.

While technical analysis basically tells us that everything is discounted and reflected in the stock's price. Stock prices move in trends and fluctuates.

After the **crash of 1987,** it took 2 years for the market to recapture back its peak level that was lost. And after the **1929 crash**, it took more than 20 years for the DOW to recapture its peak level.

Things To Know

What is a stock—It is the outstanding capital of a corporation, represented by shares, a form of ownership and is traded in a market called the stock market. The stock share can make money through the stock's dividend and quarterly earnings. The owners of the company shares are called shareholders.

The Exchanges—Stocks are traded in the stock exchange, a place for buying and selling them.

Brokerage Services—With day trading you go in and out quickly during the intra-day session.

Holding the stock for a few days before selling is swing trading. After opening an account with them, you are ready to trade online. They provide you with financial tools like stock quotes, alerts, watch list, charts and news. For every trade they charge you a fee. You are on your own.

Investors with lots of capital to invest, usually seek the help of wealth management firms like the big banks and hedge funds.

At the beginning of the year, investors who had their money under the full management of such entities had to pay fees. The banks collect service fees for their services regardless of the ups and downs in the market.

In **1987,** I remember buying a stock worth $3,500 at E.F. Hutton office. A 5% commission was deducted right away. Today, the commission fee they charge is between $7-$8 dollars per purchase regardless of the number of shares and some only charge $ 4 per transaction.

Book Value—It is the total value of a company's assets that shareholders would theoretically receive if a company were liquidated. It is an accounting value of a company.

Online Brokerage—An online brokerage firm is responsible for getting our order and carrying it out to buy or sell at the best price available. There are many online brokerage available ready to do business with us. Scottrade for example, only requires $ 1,000-2,000 minimum capital. For a margin account they require $ 25,000. With a margin account, you can short sell a stock. Your trading capital will be $ 50,000 on margin. The brokerage firm lend you more in which to buy securities.

Our roll over IRA, traditional IRA and SEP can all be within a brokerage account, including Roth IRA. <u>No taxes</u> are paid for any earnings up to the time of withdrawal or when one reach a certain age where a minimum required distribution every year have to be taken out. **You grow** the **money your own way**.

<u>Hypothetically</u>—During a Bullish Market, we can hold on our <u>low-buy stocks with great growth potentials to go forward</u>. Slight market correction is good and unavoidable. It makes some of our stocks to be fairly valued, unless there are some shocking news about our economy or the stock itself.

<u>Trend Reversal</u>—A good stock with a string of run ups and with a new 52-week high, is at risk of reversing <u>modestly</u>. Why?-Because of profit taking, and various derivatives—played by banks and other financial institutions. Computerize trading and high frequency trading plays a big role.

<u>Valuation</u>—The fundamental value that investors use to justify stock prices.

P.E.—Is the price paid for a share relative to the annual income and profit earned by the company per share. A low P.E. stock is generally undervalued and bullish.

PEG—PEG is an indicator of stock's potential value and growth. A lower PEG means that the stock is undervalued. N= 1-2.

PE ratio forward—If P.E. forward is lower than current P.E., earning is expected to grow in the future.

<u>**Calmness**</u>—**Don't trade with emotion.** Relax or there will be some behavioral changes in the way we perceive things. Various chemical messengers in the brain via neurotransmitter can greatly affect our perception and view of the stock. Our mind must be completely concentrated, and focused, when making an entry or exit point.

<u>**Fear**</u>—Fear is your enemy and time is your friend. Market fear is a distressing emotion aroused by an actual or impending decline in the market. Depending on the economic news, if the decline is less than 5%, don't panic, give your stock another day or two. We may be wrong in our first assumption of the situation. Take your time and give an <u>organize response.</u> Our **Intuition p**lays a big role. Sometimes with fear we sell prematurely instead of buying at a good price. <u>There has</u>

never been a correction without a buying opportunity later. It is always the flip-side of any correction.

Business News—Don't be shortsighted—"Man's reach should always exceed his grasp". Don't just look at the surface side of a picture, but try to look on all sides. Look at several websites carrying the news.

Correction—Is inevitable. **A 2%** CORRECTION is sometimes beautiful and necessary and it makes the stocks fairly valued. Market always recover from any correction. A stock down 50% need to rally **100%** to recover back its losses. If down **5%** the stock need to rally 5.2% and so forth.

Inflation—As inflation rises, so do interest rates. Demand for a particular product is increasingly faster than supply, we pay more because that product is scarce. Low interest rate supports economic growth.

Consumer Price Index—It measures the prices that consumers pay for the goods. One of the closely watched numbers regarding inflation.

Profit Taking—Wisdom is being wise in time after a profit. Sell some of your profit and keep your low buys and wait for the next cycle.

Awareness—Always be aware of the changes in the trend, and level of the stock market **Averages**,(the Dow, S&P, Nasdaq). **The level of the averages correlate with the movement of stock's prices.**

Charts—Line Charts are available at AOL, Google, and Yahoo Finance Websites, **for free**. I use Fidelity Active Trader, Scottrade, and Wizetrade.

Treasuries—The United States treasury security is government debt issued by the U.S. Department of Treasury through the Bureau of the Public Debt.

They are the debt financing instruments of the U.S. and referred simply as Treasuries. Other countries buy treasuries from us as investments.

Bond yield curve is important because it is used to predict the economic future.

Bonds—Any rise in interest rate is not good for the bond market. Bonds are very sensitive to interest rise. When rate is up, bond yield curve goes down and the price goes up vice versa.

Commodities—The liquid investment in the planet. It is another market wherein producers, manufacturers, distributors and others sell their products at a future date thru a commodity broker.

Main Street—Refers to the <u>average</u> people in the suburbs and urban areas.

Wall Street—Refers to the financial district of New York.

Penny Stocks—Don't buy penny stocks. These are speculative stocks.

Gold—The government can print bonds and money but not gold. Gold is bulky and not liquid. Traditionally, gold mining stocks rise when the equity market has fallen during periods of economic downturn.

Unlocking the Insights

Assuming that many of us over the years have less success in "beating the market", some investors can earn above average returns on their holdings.

Are you an **Intuitive** individual? **All of us are.** Clear your mind and you will be. Chances favor the prepared mind. Our Intuition communicate with us through an impulse or feeling from within our inner-self <u>prior to any decision making</u> and appropriate path to follow. I find this very helpful trading in a volatile market. It is a mysterious <u>perception</u> of truth that all of us possess and can develop.

The Marvelous Human Organ
The Brain

Intuition and the Autonomic Nervous System

The Central Nervous system. The seat of human emotion is the Limbic system.

The hypothalamus which is a part of the system regulates the autonomic nervous system. The autonomic nervous system, regulates <u>involuntary</u> actions.

It has 2 systems of nerves.

1. Sympathetic Nerves—The sympathetic stimulation <u>resulting</u> from <u>panic,</u> stress, fear, excites our body, speed up heart beat, raise blood pressure, are normally balanced by the parasympathetic.

2. Para-sympathetic Nerves (inhibitory). But sometimes, too much sympathetic stimulation cannot be handled by the inhibitory para-sympathetic system.

Therefore, **it only make sense to be relax in order to be able to make the right decision in any given situation. Calmness, mindfullness, and sometimes even meditation helps.** Intuition can only be fully functional when you are relaxed. Just focus on what you want to do, and **wait for that instinct feeling to come**. **Steve Jobs** once said, "Listen to Your Heart and Intuition" when trying to achieve something. This was in one of his commencement graduation speeches.

Perception

Perception—The act of understanding through our senses. It is an immediate or <u>intuitive</u> appreciation of any given situation crossing our mind.

Reaction time is fast. The probability is high, a non-mathematical calculation.

Ex. A juicy headlines like NFLX debuts in UK and Ireland (Jan 9, 2012) The stock had been devastated for several days and then came the news about UK and Ireland. The price started to go up slowly. I waited for a few seconds and felt an inner impulse within me to buy the stock. The price was already up $2.00 when I bought 100 shares. It went up to $13.00 per share during the intra-day trading period. I was in an intuitive mode when I bought the stock.

To be aware that there is an intuitive impulse within us is truly helpful. To think that there is such a thing every time we trade, makes us calm, clear, and confident. Relying wholly on different lagging indicators should only be an added part of your <u>true</u> perception. They sometimes fail to maintain there speed and intensity. Ex. Vix CBOE Volatility Index and others.

On the contrary, when our view and assessment is not in accordance with our peception, then the probability is low. We are hesitant and not sure. We take more time analyzing the situation and we don't **rush!!** By doing this all the time, we develop the principle of achieving our goal, with gradual and non-drastic moves.

Our Intuitive Mind

Intuitive Perception—Sometimes we can see a particular situation in a way others cannot in a matter of seconds. Our brain is constantly storing informations that we percieve, feel, and experience. It is like a computer machine capable of accepting and processing data. Our mind is full of such informations.

When an **impression** crosses our cognitive mind, we react automatically in a <u>very fast manner</u> The continuous evaluation of informations in our mind, are computations that we are unaware of becomes our **Intuition,** the truth within ourselves.

The part of the brain that is closely linked to learning and memory storage is the hippocampus.

Most of the time such reaction is correct. Example: When the former fiancee of CNBC's financial analyst who later became his wife, said "Let us sell all our holdings and get the hell out of here", they were saved. She was at that time trading in another desk. In that **1987 crash,** she felt an instant subtle feeling that something big is gonna happen the next day. This was the memorable black Monday crash of 1987.

An emergency room Nurse saw something on the face of her father. She brought him right away to the emergency room. He was save from a fatal heart attack.

Any skilled professional, like a basketball or chess player can figure out and see situations in a matter of second and can adjust accordingly. This is our Intuition, an ability we all possessed but not oftenly used.

Our Intuition can become an added trading tool especially when we need to decide quickly either to enter or exit a position. This is a phenomenon that many of us had experienced.

Michael Barry a young MD, graduate from Stanford School of Medicine who successfuly managed his Scion Fund, for years, shorted the market in **2007.**

He had that feeling that the housing bubble is forthcoming. Many of his investors left the Fund but he was right after all. In 2008, he closed his fund and mainly focused on his own personal investments successfuly up to the present time.

The Results of An Early Occurrence.

When we are going to execute a given action, we can also predict its consequences. The past action model we have seen before enables such prediction. Therefore, backtracking the past price history (chart's technical) of a stock quickly is very important before buying and selling. Ex. **Sina** a Chinese stock was priced $142.83 in April 2, 2011. In Nov. 24, 2011 it was down to $ 63.51. We have seen the stock's price to fluctuates in the past.

We can predict therefore that any catalyst related to this stock will definitely make us some money, unless there is something fundamentally wrong with the stock. We just have to wait for the right time.

Theory of Probability

The probability **concept** is related to a logical and consistent decision making. It also **refer to the <u>percentage of chance</u> that someting will happen, from a random number of 0-1.(100%).** Nothing below 0 and above 1. Ex. February 2012. The gasoline and crude oil prices have gone up. The rising tension in Iran's nuclear program with Israel and the strait of Hormuz possible blockade by the Iranian became an issue. I bought Marathon Oil, based on my probability rating of USO's 10-day volume configuration chart, plus other intuitive positive insights coming from the business media. USO is a U.S. oil fund. All news are pointing towards a continued high gasoline price. But USO has been up for 10 solid days? The probability that it might reverse on the 11th day is 100%, regardless of what our motivations are. I was wrong buying MRO.

My daily Newspapers are the CNBC and Bloomberg TV. I watch it 8 hrs. a day or more. The European market news starts at 1:00 AM and the Asian market at 2:00 AM Central Time at Bloomber TV. These 2 markets, determine the direction of the U.S. future market. It tells us more or less where the averages will be at the opening and during the intra-day period.

A Reciprocal Relationship

There is a correlation between the news and the price m<u>ovement </u>of the stocks and the averages. Ex. The <u>European Credit crisis and failure of our politicians to solve our budget debt deficit, is a long term concern.</u> Any good News about the Euro dollar crisis on the other hand will be good for the market and our stocks.

Investors Sentiment

Price movements are also driven by what investors think will <u>probably </u>happen. There are millions of thoughts out there participating in the movements of the stocks.

Personal Sentiment—If you feel taking the first step is correct you don't have to see the whole staircase, just take the first step and move forward. Ex. If I strongly feel that the stock's quarterly earning reports will beat the estimate, and revenue will be good, then I will buy it.

Buying During A <u>Short Term </u>Selloff

During a short temporary sell off in the market, stick with the companies you like. Short market correction is all right. It makes some of our stocks to be fairly valued. <u>Continue holding on your low-buy stocks with high expectation potentials.</u>

You may even consider them as your <u>long term investments</u>. Don't undo your position hurriedly.

Articles, Books, andTrading Brokerage.

Extending back beyond memory, many books, articles, and innovative trading strategies have been written on technicals related to stochastic, MACD, candle volume analysis, technical indicator like Northington RSVI as a way to improve trend entry points. Carlson confirmation model, which provides a basis to determine whether the current high or low price stocks are on extremes or whether there is a new trend to be bought.

Vectorvest another unique trading tool and other wealth building workshops in options, futures, currencies tradings were likewise held and marketed for investors. Different investment firms providing us with <u>free</u> analytical report telling us where the stock's prices are headed over the next several months. Buy the most simple, best, less expensive tool (software) available out there. I use Fidelity, Scottrade and Wizetrade Trading Software. They are easy, and simple to comprehend.

Without any doubt, all these tools are helpful. Clearly there is no single tool that we can completely rely on. So, why not <u>include</u> our **Intuition,** as a psychological tool and illuminate the fog of uncertainties that surrounds the market every so often.

Time, Direction and Trend

After a Bear market, picking the bottom is difficult. The same is true after a recession. We cannot reduce the **time duration** to a point. In other words, we cannot pin point exactly where the prices will settle down and **<u>reverse.</u>**

Time and price direction is constantly moving. Even in **<u>option trading</u>**, we basically look at the put/call ratio. A large increase in call ratio signify that expectation or optimism is high. They are all probabilities and can change anytime. **However, we can trace backward the <u>price history</u> and see the fluctuation of the stock's price <u>over time</u>.**

I used Fidelity's Pro-Active trading chart consisting of 10-day time frame for my probability analysis. The 1-year chart for the top and low end of a trend

The 2-day chart for the beginning of a trend. The intra-day chart, for the price fluctuations of the day. I use Wizetrade for monitoring my 12 stocks and for momentum trading. **Yahoo's** interactive chart will likewise show us some of it.

With Fidelity to qualify for $ 8.00/trade, one must have a minimum of 250 trades a year.

Supply and Demand

The market moves on **supply and demand.** If there are more buying than selling, then the market will move up. However, you can always envision what is behind any trend. There is much more going on behind a trend that we should know like breaking news, commentaries, analysis and investment advices on a stock or market in general. Ex. Stocks slumped as Greece slogged through negotiations with other European countries over the bailout situation. The market dropped.

Yahoo's Interactive Chart

Line chart is easy and simple to comprehend. It is less tiresome than staring at complex chart-software. Complicated stock charting flat forms, makes our decision more complicated.

<u>Looking at one data point</u> is not enough. Different time periods will give us a a better perception of the stock and the market. Ex. <u>At Yahoo,</u> 1D,5D,1M.

YTD, 3M, 6M, 1-yr., 2-yr, 5-yr and Max. (Interactive chart). The point of reference: When was the stock 1-2-3-years ago or 10 days ago?

There Are Two Types of Trend

1. **The big fluctuations (Uptrend or Downtrend)**-The duration can last longer. The forces of supply and demand are too large. The swing traders likes it, and they trade at the beginning of such trend. Then sell <u>some</u> on top after 1-3 days.

2. **The small fluctuations (ripples)**—The short term trends for day trading is a difficult trend and often times driven by investor's emotion. What ever trend we deal with, we must be ready for breakout or reversal.

Factors Affecting A Trend

Trend—Is an aggregation of opinions about a stock and its direction. Market direction are driven by News.

1.) Information—News (Type and Quality)

2.) Information Processing—What analyst think <u>will happen.</u> Earning report may be good, and revenue is not. Analyst for some reason does not like it, and the stock's price fall. Conference calls and guidance are important.

Be Consistent

If we look, examine and analyze a stock chart a hundred times, the <u>same way we interpreted</u> it <u>the first time</u>, <u>correctly</u>, we can repeat it over and over again. Consistently throwing a baseball with the same grip and hand grasp and always doing it right is another good example. So winning the first time the right way can be followed with successful wins if you do it right. **Do your online trading the right way.** Avoid repeating previous mistakes. Stick to your rules.

We are what we repeatedly do.

Forecaster and Stockpicker

We can do the same if not better than what a stock picker can do. Most of the time they are just <u>predicting the past</u>. They cannot predict exactly the future trend. They are actually concluding from what had been known (past trend) and what can probably happen. They just hope that the future direction of the stock price be better than the past. They are no better than the rest of us in interpreting situation presented to them. Ex. I saw Boeing stock at $57.51 last April 2011 and in 2012, at $75.00. Boeing had just finalized its biggest plane order from Indonesia's Lion air worth $22.4 billions. When I look at the 1-year chart there was not enough room for the stock to go up, so I did not buy it.

Visit : **StockTA website** for technical analysis, whether the stock is oversold or overbought. **Shaeffer's Put /Call website**—For options activities. Options trading is an integral part of the market. We must be aware of trading activities.

Volume configuration is an easier way to look at such activities.

Actual Home Online Trading

When I wake up in the morning and before the market opens—I watch the News from (Bloomberg TV and Cnbc TV.) I don't trade with luck. As I've learned over the years the following guides are important.

Guide No.1
The Extended Hours

Preview the market outlook. Is the **futures** flat, weak or strong?. Is the economic forecast gloomy or bright? Try to figure out how the market will play at the opening bell. Likewise look at the Vix, the volatility index chart. If things does not look good and **If there is no positive market news, there may not be a good reason to trade.**

Business News—Update yourself with the early morning economic NewsTop stories, breaking news, at Aol and Google Finance web front page. Inflation and rate hike are always an important factors in the market. Quarterly earning reports, international economic news, acquisitions, mergers, Ipos, and so forth.

Ex. European stocks falls following Greece bailout concern.

A good home online trader understand that **everything is interrelated**.

If one trade equities and do not pay attention to the bond market, currency, and commodity markets as **well as everything else that is going on around the world, including perhaps the birds flapping their wings, he will not succeed. An overall daily pre-market assessment and picture of the market is**

important. When the economic news are extremely negative, and the averages are down big, figure out which sector will be hit hard. Rationalize the situation and be ready to respond appropriately but if you panic, you become disconnected.

Guide No. 2
Be A Great Market and Economic <u>Data</u> Watcher

1. **<u>Economic Indicators</u>**—Durable good orders, factory orders, housing construction, new home sales, automobile sales, **gross domestic products**, (GDP), durable goods, consumers price index, jobless claims, and so forth.

2. **<u>Inflation Indicators</u>**—Interest rates, producer's price index, consumers spending, gold, oil, employment index, personal and consumers spending, CRB commodity research bureau and so forth.

3. **<u>Fed and Fiscal Policies.</u>** What the Fed, Congress, and Senate are doing in relation to our economy. Federal Reserve Board sets monetary policy to ensure, that there is enough money and <u>credit</u> available to sustain economic growth. The Fed always sees to it that inflation is under control.

4. **International News**—The global economy. Ex. European Credit Crisis.

Guide No. 3
Using the Line Chart

I use the line chart and not the candle stick (Japanese). I prefer a chart that is simple and easy to understand. It provides the general price overview on a stock. Trend lines analysis at its best are considered by many as an inexact science. During the intra-day period, anything can happen. Use our perception, the one thing necessary toward a worthwhile achievement.

The **2-day trading chart** (Frequency 1-minute)—**9:30 AM** (Central time) will clearly show us the opening trend whether up or down. If it is upward, I will wait for the second uptrend around **10:AM,** which is a buy most of the time.

Then I follow the trend, in the intra-day period up to the closing. I'll keep an eye on any big changes. Any small fluctuations is not alarming, but a big drop is. You need a simple chart for monitoring the trend. Entry points are important.

Most of the time we buy too early. Haste make waste. Let the stock's price fluctuate for a while before buying.

Note: Line Charts (interactive, basic technical analysis) all available for **FREE** at Yahoo, Google, Aol, and other sites. But of course, you don't just buy on technical analysis alone.

Intra-day Chart—If I am late in buying a stock following a good news, **I will not chase the stock.** Instead, I will focus on the intra-day price movements and find a good entry point. If I cannot do it, I will just **abstain.**

Guide No. 4
The Nucleus and Center of My Trading Activity Revolves Around the Intra-day Direction of My Stocks and Business News.

Even if the pre-market averages are down big, following Standard and Poor downgrading of 7 European banks, our non-financial holdings may not be affected at all. Ex. Amyln Pharmaceutical company, is a bio-tech company.

Although it is impossible to know what to expect from the market's daily behavior, we can still <u>percieve</u> what can happen during the intra-day trend, based on our perception of important news headlines.

Guide No. 5
Top End and Bottom End

There is something <u>more important than the News</u> and that is to be able to <u>percieve</u> the <u>beginning and the end of a trend.</u> We sell at the top and buy at the bottom.

Ex. Any turn around in the housing market after 4 years, is a reversal from the bottom.

Guide No. 6
Business Media

Business reports by journalists are sometimes **tinted with guess-work, incomplete and limited in its content. Sometimes, they narrate it in a different way. Ex. A flip-flop self-proclaim analyst** who makes daily recommendations more on what stock to buy, than what to sell and who sells his books, and enttertainment gimmicks on television regardless whether our economy is looking gloomy or bright.

Guide No. 7
News Processing, Filtering, and Analyzing

News headlines—(Positive or negative news) How will the market react to it?

Will it make a big splash in the pool or just create short ripples effect? Read between the lines. Look at the whole picture. Don't just look at the surface view. Go deeper. Ex. On Feb.7, 2012, **Apple,** the number one company in the world by market capitalization suddenly dropped. Why? Do your homework.

On Mar. 6, 2012, I bought Apple stock. On March 9, at 2:00 PM (central time) Greece had officially defaulted on its debts to private lenders. Like I said, I never hold too long on any stocks. But after reviewing thoroughly the news, I kept it and the stock went up another 6 points ($ 555.15 Monday-Mar.12) from my original buy of $ 528.00 on March 6, 2012. On March 13/2012, the stock continue to go up another 11.24 points rising to $ 563.47 per share. The psychological level is already high. A 5 days of consistent uptrend. I will be careful. At this point it will be impossible to short the stock. It can also swing downward. I will be relax, focus and concentrated so I can create an appropriate environment through which my inner perception can function appropriately analyzing the situation.

Guide No. 8
Averages
(Dow, S&P 500, Nasdaq)

From a trading perspective, one must always **be guided by the averages** especially the DOW. **The movement of the stock is correlated and moves in tandem with level of the averages.**

For every "real time tick" of the average levels, the stock prices change too. The right level is determined by the present condition in our economy and news headlines. Try to recognize a major price reversal following a 52-week high in your stock or the averages.

Any pull back or breakout below this level and any break out above such level, will determined your move.

If the market is very unpredictable and volatile <u>don't trade</u>.

Stay on the side and wait for another opportunity.

Guide No. 9
Don't Hurry

On any breaking News which is a common occurrence, don't hurry, take your time, and get a good entry point. Stock prices fluctuate. On any rumors, you may or may not buy the stock. Good intuition and judgment is important.

Rumors like merger, acquisition, and others sometimes amount to nothing.

Guide No. 10
Catalyst

Buy a stock when there is a <u>catalyst,</u> and when the 1-year chart shows us that the stock has been declining for awhile.

On the contrary, if the 10-day daily chart was already up for 3-4 days, then it may not be a buying opportunity for me. The trend may or may not reverse. However, a 10-day uptrend will definitely reverse. Profits have to be taken out by the traders.

The period covering from 8:30 AM-10:00 AM (Central Time) is a guide for the <u>initial</u> direction of the stock. The intra-day chart, is a guide if the uptrend will be sustainable or not.

Guide No. 11
Quarterly Earning Reports By Companies

Earning numbers reported, are sometimes not trustworthy. It is more often unreliably based on calls of doubtful quality. Instead, look at the cash flow statements, the cash moving in and out of the business. It must be of high quality.

Guide No. 12
Short Selling and Covering

Short selling and short covering are <u>common activities</u> in the market.

The purpose of using these strategies is to perform well in a weak market and have the edge during strong market. It is therefore important to know the following: a.) No. of shares <u>held short</u> in **percentage %**—Calculated by dividing No. of shares shorted by the No. of shares outstanding. b.) Short interest ratio—is calculated by the No. of shares shorted divided by the average daily trading volume. High value is bearish and low value is bullish. c.) Comparing current shares shorted to those prior, will tell us any increase (worsening) or decrease (improvement) or <u>reversal</u> in trend. Available **FREE**—Short Interest Data website.

Let us not be a victim of our own success by rushing to buy more stocks after winning a few. Hold on to stocks only for a few days. Don't **be too greedy** get out when you have profit and not to keep hoping for the stock price to go up higher.

Sell 2/3 and keep 1/3 of your shares for a possible long term hold. This is especially true for hot, growth, momentum stocks. If the economy is bullish, then be a <u>long term</u> investor.

Guide No. 13
Pre-Market Assessment of My holdings
Index Versus Ultra short

Before the market opens, I usually like to see an overall picture of the market on my computer screen. Movements of the stock's prices have to be analyzed in relation to any negative or positive events. Ex. Crude Oil—If I am worried about any pullback, I will monitor USO the U.S. Oil Fund <u>versus </u>DUG, the Pro shares ultra short oil and gas ETF. In financial it will be XLF, the financial select sector index <u>versus</u> SKF or Faz.—Proshares Ultrashort Financials, correspond to the daily <u>inverse</u> performance of the Dow Jones U.S. Financial Index.

The Dow Jones Industrial Average ETF DIA Index <u>versus</u> the Ultra short Dow 30 Etf Proshares.

Our Positive Thoughts

You don't just stumble into the future. You create your own future. Feel good and positive. Whatever you are thinking now becomes your future. Shift your emotions to feeling good and positiveness. Visualize and it will materialize.

Focus on what you want and it will happen. You are the master of your own life.

We have several thousands of thoughts a day. Choose the thoughts that will make you feel better, gaining and not losing.

Keeping Ourselves Busy

A retentive memory is a good thing, and such ability is a blessing. As we grow old, senile dementia becomes a problem to many of us. It is the loss of cognitive ability beyond what may be expected from normal aging. To fight it is a token of greatness. Scientists, researchers, medical authorities said that m<u>ental activity, exercise and right diet </u>is at the present time the only way to delay the onset of this aging process.

Trading online can be a part of our lifestyle in retirement. It keep us busy everyday. As long as we can keep ourselves busy, find new ways to look into, we don't get old very fast.

Just recently, on the 84th Academy Award, Christopher Plummer at age 82 won his first Oscar as supporting actor in the movie the "Beginners".

In these tough economic times, people about to retire and baby boomers are sometimes worried that they may not enjoy their golden years ahead. I always say this because of our government's 16 trillion dollar debts. It makes investment tough. Such enormous debts is a growing concern to many baby boomers and their children.

To the beginners—Winning starts from the beginning. Be ready before you go out there to the investment world. The stock market serves as a playground for those who are enthusiastic to venture, make money and do what others have done.

Manuel T. Prospero, MD

To the online traders it is important to be current on what is happening in our <u>economy, domestically and internationally</u>. They interrelate with the market.

Let us be a good listener. Our ears will never get us in trouble. Let our heart and Intuition guide us. It whispers, so let us listen carefully.

Likewise, our determination plays a very important role during our journey to financial success. It is how we look at things and how they will be confronting us.

Only then can we become a good investor.

If there is a better way to do it . . . find it . . .

Note: For further assistance: E-mail us at: **Pmisterstocks @ Aol.com or Gianter@Aol.com.** Thank you.

End

www.ingramcontent.com/pod-product-compliance
Lightning Source LLC
Chambersburg PA
CBHW021036180526
45163CB00005B/2150